{ CITIESCAPE }

DELHI*

{ CITIESCAPE }

SARINA SINGH

CONTENTS*

VITAL
STATS*

{ **NAME** Delhi **DATE OF BIRTH** 500 BC. }
Historical evidence indicates settlement at about this
time. Delhi has had many incarnations, with at least
eight major powers building their capital here. The
final Delhi, New Delhi, was constructed by the British,
becoming the capital of independent India in 1947.
HEIGHT 218m **SIZE** 1483 sq km **ADDRESS** India
POPULATION 12.8 million

7.

PEOPLE*

{ *** THE INDIAN CAPITAL IS A MISCELLANY OF ETHNIC GROUPS AND RELIGIONS, WITH HINDUS ACCOUNTING FOR THE LARGEST SLICE** of the population pie by far. There's a sizeable community of Sikhs and Muslims, and also expatriates, as Delhi is the base for numerous foreign diplomatic missions. Hindi, Urdu, Punjabi and English are the most widely spoken languages. With its Hindu majority, the caste system is still evident in Delhi – although it's not as prevalent as in rural India – and Brahmins occupy the top spot. }

RELIGION AND FAMILY lie at the core of society and despite the growing number of nuclear families, the extended family remains a cornerstone in Delhi. Men, usually the breadwinners, are also generally considered the head of the household. Most Delhiites marry in their twenties, and while the past decade has seen a climbing number of 'love marriages', arranged marriages are still the norm.

9.

ANATOMY*

{ *** ALTHOUGH IT'S SOMEWHAT SPREAD OUT – URBAN SPRAWL IS RIFE – DELHI IS A RELATIVELY STRAIGHTFORWARD CITY TO NAVIGATE.** The Yamuna River twists around the capital's northeastern precincts and the city is dotted with green patches such as leafy Lodi Garden and the forested ridge west of Rashtrapati Bhavan. }

THERE ARE TWO main sections: Old Delhi and New Delhi. New Delhi is spacious and planned; its heart is the vast shop-and-restaurant-laden traffic circle known as Connaught Place. In stark contrast is action-packed Old Delhi to the north – famed for its historic Mughal architecture, most notably the Red Fort and Jama Masjid. Old Delhi's main artery is the chronically congested Chandni Chowk.

STILL, GETTING AROUND the city is a breeze once you've mastered the art of local taxi and rickshaw fare-setting. There's no dearth of autorickshaws, cycle-rickshaws, taxis and buses, and there's also a modern metro system.

PERSON ALITY*

{

* THE CAPITAL OF THE WORLD'S SECOND-MOST POPULOUS NATION, DELHI IS WITHOUT A DOUBT ONE OF ASIA'S MOST ENIGMATIC AND CAPTIVATING CITIES.
Regardless of how many times you visit, and no matter how convinced you may be that you've peeled back the skin of this multi-layered city, there are always more layers underneath. Demystifying Delhi seems to be a perpetual work-in-progress and that's precisely what makes it so intensely memorable, so deeply addictive.

THIS GUTSY CITY has endured a long history of conquering armies, bloody resistance, fleeing populations and itinerant traders, having been singled out as a desired capital by at least eight major powers. As a result, Delhi's construction has been a patchwork affair, with each ruler opting to build anew rather than add to an existing city. The city doesn't have a single defining persona, but rather a conglomeration of disparate identities that reflect not only a kaleidoscopic history, but also a jumble of inhabitants.

13.

Serving as North India's major international gateway, Delhi's exposure to people from different nationalities and walks of life has also played a hand in making it the cosmopolitan city you see today: tolerant, creative, quick to adapt, tenacious and with an amazing capacity for reinvention.

YOU DON'T HAVE to peer through a magnifying glass to see this incredible diversity, the city oozes with it: the Sikh gurdwara (temple) standing a stone's throw away from the Hindu temple; the huge Western-style shopping mall looming over the little Ayurvedic apothecary. When hunger strikes, Delhi delights with delicious menu items, thanks to the locals' love of eating out and their willingness to try new things. It's hardly surprising that Delhi is described as one of India's tastiest towns.

DELHI LOVES TO CELEBRATE. Go wild at a thumping nightclub, where the sons and daughters of the elite come out to play. Witness a festival, always celebrated with intense passion and devotion, an exhilarating mix of spirituality, colour and noise. Accept a box of mithai, Indian sweets that come in a fantastical array of shapes, textures and colours. (So many of these rich, sugary sweets are given away at the Diwali festival that apparently many of Delhi's sweet-makers are admitted to hospital after it, suffering exhaustion.)

DELHI ISN'T A place you merely 'see': this city's an all-enveloping sensory roller-coaster ride that will leave you bamboozled, ecstatic, bemused and inspired all at once. With one foot grounded in venerated traditions and the other passionately bounding into the e-age, Delhi straddles the old and the new with gritty gumption, a dexterous balancing act which hasn't by any means been achieved in the wink of an eye. Explore the city further in the chapters that follow: spiritual, dynamic, charming and overwhelming, there's a whole lot more to India's capital than meets the eye.

14.

SPIRITUAL*

{ *NO MATTER WHERE YOU VENTURE IN DELHI, YOU'LL SOON FIND YOURSELF UP-CLOSE-AND-PERSONAL WITH SOMETHING SPIRITUAL.** Everyday life is intimately intertwined with the sacred: the housewife devoutly performing puja (prayer) each morning at a tiny shrine in her home, the seemingly rupee-worshipping shopkeeper who nevertheless ignores the eager-to-buy customers until after blessings have been sought from the gods. Most Delhiites are Hindu, and the city's numerous Hindu temples range from elaborate structures based on auspicious ancient architectural styles to tiny banyan-shaded shrines lovingly set up by street urchins. Devotion has no social boundaries. }

DELHI IS also home to a sizable Muslim and Sikh population, and has a number of positively breathtaking mosques and gurdwaras. The Jama Masjid (Islamic) and Gurdwara Bangla Sahib (Sikh), for instance, never fail to leave you tingling no matter how many times you visit.

17.

ALTHOUGH HINDUISM, ISLAM AND SIKHISM – Delhi's dominant faiths – may tread different spiritual paths, they all attract pan-social-strata devotion, which means you'll find dhobi-wallahs and business tycoons praying side by side at any of the city's temples, gurdwaras or mosques.

A RECENT ARCHITECTURAL marvel is the amazing Bahai Temple, dedicated to public worship in 1986. This house of worship represents the Bahai faith: divine in origin, all-embracing in scope, broad in its outlook, scientific in its method, humanitarian in its principles and dynamic in its influence. One of the youngest of the world's independent religions, Bahai's founder, Bahaullah (1817–92), is regarded by Bahais as the most recent in the line of Messengers of God. The central theme is that humanity is one single race and that the day has come for its unification into one global society.

APART FROM WORSHIP, physical and mental purification is also considered a fundamental means of attaining spiritual harmony, and is commonly pursued via meditation and yoga. A small but powerfully charged word lies at the centre of many Indian meditation styles: 'Om'. Said to be the sound of the universe, this sacrosanct Hindu and Buddhist invocation represents the essence of the Divine. For Hindus, 'Om' symbolises the creation, maintenance and destruction of the universe and thus the holy Hindu Trimurti of the gods Brahma, Vishnu and Shiva. It is repeatedly chanted to achieve a state of complete emptiness, complete serenity.

WELCOME TOO to Delhi the karma capital – a city where the ancient and revered notions of karma, samsara (reincarnation), dharma (moral code of behaviour) and moksha (liberation) are very much alive.

SOUL FOOD*

{ * **INDIA'S FAST-PACED CAPITAL IS EMBRACING GLOBALISATION WITH GUSTO,** but in stark contrast to the material marathon of the 21st century, ancient practices that accelerate spiritual growth are being ardently pursued as well. A skyrocketing number of people are making meditation and yoga part of their daily life – whether it's a meditation session with friends at a neighbourhood park or a formal yoga class at a swanky suburban gym. }

SOME INDIANS say this hunger for spiritual sustenance is a result of the work-hard-play-hard attitude that has emerged as the new mantra for today's youth. Others say it's mimicking the West, where meditation and yoga have achieved pop-star status – a droll idea considering that most meditation and yoga styles have their roots in India.

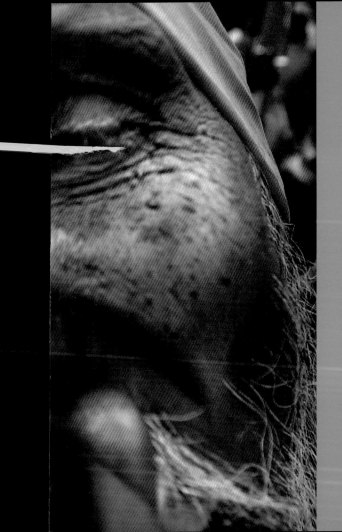

HINDU HOLY MEN surrender all material possessions to seek spiritual enlightenment through meditation, the study of sacred texts, self-mortification and pilgrimage. Known as sadhus, they survive by receiving food and money from others, and good karma is bestowed on those who behave with generosity toward them. Sadhus are deeply interconnected with the Divine: Lord Shiva, a prominent Hindu deity, is often characterised as a Himalaya-dwelling ascetic with matted hair, ash-smeared body and a third eye symbolising wisdom.

HINDU DEITIES*

{ * **HINDUISM HAS NO FOUNDER, YET IS ONE OF THE PLANET'S OLDEST AND MOST MIND-STIRRING RELIGIONS.** After all, which other faith can lay claim to such a large number of deities? Hindus believe in Brahman, the ultimate reality and the source of all existence, from which everything emanates and to which everything will ultimately return. Though all of the multitude of deities are regarded as manifestations of Brahman, there are three main representations: Brahma, creator of the universe; Vishnu, protector of all that is good in the world; and Shiva, the destroyer without whom creation couldn't occur. }

BRAHMAN HAS NO attributes, but all the other gods, the manifestations, do. Hindu gods and goddesses commonly worshipped in Delhi include jolly elephant-headed Ganesh, the god of good fortune; Krishna, an incarnation of Vishnu; Durga, who is the mother and destroyer of evil; and Lakshmi, the goddess of wealth.

WITH DOMES SOARING skyward, Delhi's large Lakshmi Narayan Temple (commonly known as Birla Mandir) was inaugurated in 1938 by the father of the nation, Mahatma Gandhi. He stipulated that all members of the community, including untouchables, be allowed to worship here. The red sandstone complex was built by BD Birla, a prosperous Indian industrialist whose family has erected many temples around India. It is dedicated to Lakshmi, the Hindu goddess of wealth, and her consort, Narayan the Preserver.

WHAT GOES AROUND*

{ *** IF YOU'RE WHIZZING THROUGH DOWNTOWN DELHI IN A RICKSHAW AND SUDDENLY FIND YOURSELF FACE DOWN** in a puddle of murky water after colliding with a bus, don't be surprised if a well-meaning Delhiite reassures you that the bingle was no coincidence. No, no, it was your karma. A karmic debt has left you drinking drain water on that pothole-riddled road. }

HINDUS BELIEVE that earthly life is cyclical, and that you are born again and again, the quality of these rebirths dependent upon your karma in previous lives. It's a concept that can turn life into a whole new ball game for karma greenhorns. If you believe that your conduct and actions in this lifetime will have repercussions in your future lives, you start to tread carefully. 'Wrong' choices made today could well come back to bite you tomorrow!

30.

SIKHING EQUALITY *

{ * **SIKHISM WAS FOUNDED BY GURU NANAK IN THE 15TH CENTURY IN PUNJAB TO AMALGAMATE ELEMENTS OF HINDUISM AND ISLAM,** the subcontinent's two major – and warring – religions of that time. Sikhism has ten gurus; Delhi's Gurdwara Bangla Sahib is an especially significant temple because it was built at the place where the eighth guru, Harkrishan Dev, spent several months in 1664. This guru dedicated most of his time to helping the destitute and sick and was revered for his extraordinary healing powers; a tank on the gurdwara's premises contains water which is believed to have curative properties. }

A BELIEF IN THE equality of all beings lies at the heart of Sikhism. It's expressed in various practices, including langar, whereby people from all walks of life – regardless of caste and creed – sit side by side to share a complimentary meal prepared by volunteers in the gurdwara's communal kitchen.

IRRESIS TIBLE*

{ *** DELHI OFFERS A SUMPTUOUS BANQUET OF FOOD – LUSCIOUS FLAVOURS, FLAMBOYANT COLOURS, HEAVENLY AROMAS** and fantastical textures. From southern vegetarian recipes to the meaty fare of the Mughals and the Euro-Indian fusions of erstwhile colonies, there's something from almost every pocket of the subcontinent here. Delhi's diverse cuisine is partly a reflection of its assorted ethnic population, the result of the constant stream of people from around the country coming to seek success in the big city. It's also, however, a result of the locals' growing desire to dabble with something different – indeed, in Delhi's society circles it's all about being seen eating something that screams international gourmet! }

THE ARRAY OF gastronomic offerings includes to-die-for Punjabi curries and melt-in-the-mouth tandoori tikkas, marvellous Mediterranean fare, crispy wood-fired pizzas and a host of wok-tossed Chinese favourites.

THE CITY also gets a resounding round of applause for its gamut of eateries, which range from the ultra-elegant to the utterly ramshackle. But regardless of their outward appearance, all take great pride in their food, whether it's a simple chickpea curry at a roadside dhaba (snack bar), or velvety caramel custard in a hotel restaurant.

YOU CAN KICK off the day with a breakfast of South Indian idlis, North Indian parathas or American-style buttermilk pancakes, followed by a lunch of Mughlai curry, Tibetan thupka or Northwest Frontier-style kebabs. For afternoon tea, possibilities include Austrian-style apple strudel, authentic Bengali mithai (sweets) or French-inspired crème caramel. Then for dinner there's everything from Punjabi butter chicken to Thai green curry to parmesan-sprinkled mushroom risotto – all beautifully washed down with a glass of Belgian beer, Indian rum or Australian chardonnay.

BACK IN THE HOME KITCHEN, daily staples include rice, chapati and dhal, usually accompanied by a selection of sabzi (vegetable) dishes that are either cooked sukhi (dry) or tari (sauce-based).

AND OF COURSE there are the mouthwatering mithai, divinely wicked goodies that can make an appearance at almost any time of the day. A must for any auspicious occasion is a sweet like the golden-yellow motichoor ladoo, a delicacy of sugar, cardamom and pistachio. During Diwali countless boxes of mithai are distributed – it's said that around five million barfis, two million gulab jamuns and one million ladoos alone are sold in the capital during this time. This may explain the swelling obesity problem and the spiralling number of dental clinics!

BETWEEN MEALS, a favourite practice is the chewing of paan (a mixture of betel nut and leaves) for its stimulant effects, to satisfy hunger and also to freshen the breath. Paan comes in different varieties, including a number containing tobacco.

STREET EATS*

{ * **MORNING, NOON AND NIGHT YOU'LL FIND ROADSIDE VENDORS FRYING, BOILING, ROASTING OR SIMMERING THINGS TO LURE PECKISH PASSERS-BY.** }
Popular eats include bhajia, chaat and aloo tikka, but the king of all street snacks would have to be the samosa, a delicious vegetable-stuffed deep-fried pastry triangle.

THEN THERE ARE Delhi's indefatigable omelette-wallahs, precariously pushing egg-laden carts through the crush of mechanical and human traffic, ever ready to whisk, fry and flip.

ISLAMIC-INFLUENCED Old Delhi has a particularly enticing street-food scene, with specialities including fried masala fish and kebabs, the latter often doused in curd and wrapped in warm paratha (layered bread). In Old Delhi there's even a special lane dedicated purely to paratha, Paratha Wali Gali; the bread comes either stuffed with spiced fillings or simply smothered with ghee.

PAAN-WALLAHS do a roaring trade. These traders deftly mix the sweet, spicy and fragrant concoction of betel nut, lime paste and assorted condiments into a silky paan leaf.

LEGEND SAYS that Buddha once cut his eyelids off in an act of penance for falling asleep during meditation. The lids grew into tea plants which, when brewed, banished sleep. Today chai (tea) is as revered as ever, with Delhiites drinking an average of 1680 cups each per year.

NAAN BETTER*

{ * **LYING IN THE HEARTLAND OF NORTH INDIA, IT'S REALLY NO SURPRISE THAT DELHI SHINES WHEN IT COMES TO REGIONAL NORTHERN SPECIALITIES** like lip-smacking Punjabi curries and Mughlai dishes. Peek into a Delhi home and you're likely to see a pot of dhal bubbling on the stove, along with a bevy of North-Indian-style curried vegetables such as aloo gobi, saag and baigan. The carnivorous family may also have meat-based curries. }

DELHIITES HAVE MORE of a penchant for bread than rice, although both are often offered, with the rice and dhal usually eaten together at the conclusion of the meal. However, when it comes to mopping up every last drop of curry sauce, nothing matches a piping hot chapati freshly flipped off the tawa. Flaky paratha and deep-fried, puffed-up poori are usually eaten on special occasions or when guests are invited to dinner.

DOSA-LICIOUS*

{ *** THE CAPITAL'S FETISH FOR REGIONALLY DIVERSE CUISINE HAS DRAWN SOUTH-INDIAN CHEFS TO THE CITY** to woo hungry Delhiites with the iconic savoury pancake, the mighty dosa, as well as other southern specialities. Not so long ago, Delhi's South-Indian options were largely confined to the ubiquitous masala dosa (filled with potato), but nowadays more and more menus are flaunting lesser-known varieties such as rava dosa (made with semolina batter) and paneer dosa (stuffed with cheese). Idlis, vadas and uttapams are also being gobbled up in record numbers. }

FED UP with their inability to match the prowess of their South-Indian brothers, a handful of disgruntled North-Indian chefs have defied tradition and brazenly ventured into uncharted dosa territory. The chocolate banana dosa offered by one Delhi eatery is, however, nothing short of a travesty, according to dosa traditionalists – tantamount to making a chocolate banana omelette.

SPICE IT UP*

{ *** DELHIITES FEAST ON SOME OF THE WORLD'S FINEST CURRIES, THANKS TO THE TREMENDOUS VARIETY OF FRESHLY GROUND SPICES** and masala blends available. A curry is usually born with the crackle of cumin seeds in sizzling hot oil; subsequent flavour-boosters include cardamom, coriander seeds, turmeric and cloves. Other ingredients used are garlic, ginger and onion; chilli – slivered or powdered – is added in varying quantities depending on how much 'fire' the chef desires. }

SAFFRON is less commonly used, not only because of its high price, but also due to the risk of unknowingly buying the adulterated variety, aptly nicknamed 'bastard saffron' (usually diluted with safflower). The authentic saffron – the dried stigmas of crocus flowers grown in Kashmir – is so light that it takes more than 1500 hand-plucked flowers to yield just one gram.

SWEETS
FOR THE SWEET*

{ *** DELHI IS HOPELESSLY ADDICTED TO SWEETS. NOT ONLY DO THE LOCALS LOVE THE TASTE, THEY LOVE THE LOOK –** so much so that each year three tonnes of pure silver are converted into edible foil to decorate the city's sweets. Take the Lahori barfi: fat squares of thickened milk with pistachios, cardamom and rich flavourings. It's covered with real silver. The taste will bowl you over, but the look makes it the perfect gift. Then there's the cashew star cake, a round flat mix of dry fruits and nuts, laced with honey and decorated with marzipan stars – covered in silver. }

THE SWEETS COVERED in icing sugar will still tickle your tastebuds though – the kaju and kesar paans, heart-shaped cakes made from cashews, saffron and sugar; churma ladoos made from pure ghee; or the kesari pedas, round yellow delicacies with the subtle flavours of saffron and dried fruits. For the seriously sweet-toothed, there are gulab jamuns, balls of flour and powdered milk drowning in large vats of gooey home-made syrup.

CAPTIVATING*

{ * **DELHI HAS PLAYED A PIVOTAL PART IN THE COUNTRY'S HISTORY, AS IT HAS ALWAYS BEEN A GATEWAY CITY,** built on the plains near a fording point on the Yamuna River and on the route between western and central Asia and Southeast Asia. Over the centuries, Delhi has had at least eight known major powers make it their capital. }

LEGEND HAS IT that Delhi's first incarnation was the settlement of Indraprastha. Featuring in the great epic, the *Mahabharata*, Indraprastha was centred near present-day Delhi's Purana Qila (Old Fort). In fact, the first four cities of Delhi were to the south, around the area where the Qutb Minar now stands.

THE FIFTH DELHI, Firozabad, was at Firoz Shah Kotla, located in present-day New Delhi; the sixth was at Purana Qila. The Mughal emperor, Shah Jahan, built the seventh Delhi in the 17th century, thus moving the Mughal capital from Agra to Delhi; his Shahjahanabad roughly corresponds to today's Old Delhi.

53.

THE WALLED CITY of Shahjahanabad was surrounded by a sturdy defensive wall, only fragments of which now exist, and was one of the region's most prominent centres. The Kashmiri Gate, standing at the northern end of the walled city, was the scene of desperate fighting when the British retook Delhi during the 1857 Indian freedom movement.

THE EIGHTH and final city, New Delhi, was constructed by the British, who moved the capital of British India here from independence-seeking Kolkata. This move was announced in 1911 but construction was not completed, and the city officially inaugurated, until 1931. In 1947, when the British were booted out of the subcontinent, Delhi became the official capital of independent India.

THE OLD EMPIRES didn't tend to conform to natural boundaries or use present-day frontiers, and the limits of the Delhi-centred empires waxed and waned with the power of the ruler. However all of the former cities contributed to a surviving and captivating legacy of culture and richness, despite frequent invasion and destruction by Central Asian and Persian rulers, and British colonisation.

THIS LEGACY can be seen in places like the extraordinary Qutb Minar complex, with its Iron Pillar. This pillar has not rusted over the centuries, an amazing metallurgical feat. Then there's the tomb of the Mughal emperor Humayun, a grand structure built in red sandstone bordered with white and black marble. And the contribution of past empires is acknowledged in structures like the India Gate, at the centre of New Delhi, rising from a large expanse of lush green lawns where people picnic or sit in the lit areas on summer evenings.

THE TANGLED WEB *

{ *INDIA'S HISTORY – PARTICULARLY IN DELHI – HAS BEEN ONE OF GREAT CIVILISATIONS AND MULTIPLE RELIGIONS.** In the words of independent India's first prime minister, Jawaharlal Nehru, it has proved itself time and time again to be 'a bundle of contradictions held together by strong but invisible threads'. The city boasts a legacy of striking monuments – Hindu temples, Sikh gurdwaras, Islamic mosques and Jain temples – testifying to the intricate religious web that has been part of Delhi's momentous and ever-evolving life for centuries. }

TODAY, one of the most endearing aspects of the city's sacred sites is that the majority warmly welcome adherents of all faiths – something that has played a key role in fostering tolerance and harmony in this religiously diverse metropolis.

A 14-YEAR WORK of art, the 17th-century Jama Masjid is India's largest mosque and the final architectural magnum opus of Shah Jahan, of Taj Mahal fame. This massive mosque, with its three gateways, four angle towers and two minarets standing 40 metres high, attracts devotees from around the planet. The direction of Mecca, which the faithful face when praying, is indicated by the placement of the mihrab, a semicircular space under the central dome. It's reserved for the imam leading the prayers.

THE LEANING TOWER OF DELHI*

{ *ONE OF THE MOST MIND-BOGGLING STRUCTURES IN THE QUTB MINAR COMPLEX IS THE SEVEN-METRE-HIGH IRON PILLAR** raised in memory of Chandragupta II, who ruled from AD 375 to 413. The iron in this pillar is exceptionally pure – scientists remain in the dark about how the iron, which has not rusted in 1600 years, could have been cast using the technology of the time. }

THE QUTB MINAR ITSELF is a soaring victory tower that stands almost 73 metres high, tapering from a 15-metre-diameter base to just 2.5 metres at the top. There are a total of five storeys – Qutb-ud-din, the sultan who initiated the project, was eager to see the tower rise before his eyes, but sadly only lived until the completion of the first storey. It was finished by his successors, then in 1368 Firoz Shah replaced the top storey with two more and added a cupola, which crashed down in an earthquake in 1803. The tower now leans about 60 centimetres off the vertical, but it has otherwise worn the centuries remarkably well.

60.

REST IN PEACE*

{ *** CREDIT FOR HUMAYUN'S TOMB, THIS GLORIOUS PIECE OF ARCHITECTURE, GOES TO HUMAYUN'S SENIOR WIDOW HAJI BEGUM.** It was built nine years after his death in 1565 (or fourteen years after his death according to the manuscript of an 18th-century text). Humayun, the second Mughal emperor, ruled from 1530 to 1556. He was the son of the founder of the exalted Mughal line, Babur, a descendant of Genghis Khan. The tomb, in a typical Mughal garden divided by causeways, channels and pathways, is an example of the style of the wonderfully peaceful garden-tomb which culminated in the Taj Mahal at Agra. }

IT'S THE FIRST substantial example of Mughal architecture, with high arches and a double dome. The lofty mausoleum is located in the centre of the enclosure and rises from a podium of cells with arched openings; the central octagonal chamber contains the cenotaph, its openings closed off by perforated screens.

HOLDING
THE FORT *

{ *** THE MASSIVE LAL QILA (RED FORT) TODAY STANDS FORLORNLY, A SANDSTONE CARCASS.** When Emperor Shah Jahan paraded out of the fort atop an elephant into the streets of Old Delhi, though, he and the fort he built were a magnificent display of pomp and power. Shah Jahan started building in 1638 and completed the fort in 1648. The moat, which has been bone-dry since 1857, was originally crossed on creaky wooden drawbridges, but these were replaced with stone bridges in 1811. }

THE FORT'S MAIN GATE, Lahore Gate, is a potent symbol of modern India. During the fight for independence from British rule, there was a nationalist aspiration to see the Indian flag flying over the gate – that dream became reality. Since independence many landmark political speeches have taken place at the fort, and every year on Independence Day (15 August) it hosts the prime minister's address to the nation.

66.

PURANA QILA*

{ * **THE 16TH-CENTURY PURANA QILA (OLD FORT) WAS STARTED BY HUMAYUN BUT COMPLETED BY SHER SHAH,** the Afghan ruler who briefly interrupted Mughal rule by defeating Humayun. This magnificent monument reveals the delicate taste of both emperors, with its deeply red sandstone and exquisitely carved marble. The 4-metre-thick walls rise to 20 metres high in places, and make a circuit of almost 2 kilometres, with each corner featuring a massive bastion. It's believed that it was built on the site of Indraprastha, the capital city of the Pandavas, who were the first major power to settle in the region. }

AS FATE WOULD have it, when Humayun recaptured control of his city he slipped down the stairs of one of the towers that Sher Shah had built, and sustained injuries from which he later died.

DYNAMIC*

{ **WITH ITS ECLECTIC ETHNICITY, DELHI IS A HEAD-SPINNING MELTING POT OF CULTURES, CUSTOMS, LANGUAGES, ART FORMS,** spiritual beliefs and culinary traditions. One of the capital's most enigmatic features is its astounding diversity, with the contrast of old and new evident around almost every corner. Open-air bazaars crammed along the twisting alleys of Old Delhi flog their home-made herbal potions and essential oils, while just a short rickshaw ride away ostentatious shopping centres sell Christian Dior sunglasses and Lacoste shirts. }

IN 21ST-CENTURY DELHI, the juxtaposition of time-revered and New Age flies in the face of some common stereotypes. Sure you'll find tandoori chicken and women decked out in technicoloured saris, but these days your tandoori chicken may well come atop a cheesy wood-fired pizza, and that reticent-looking sari-clad lady you pass on the street may be chatting about last night's re-run of *Sex and the City* on a state-of-the-art mobile phone that makes yours look like a fossil.

71.

IN CONTRAST TO daylight hours, when Delhi's streets swarm with people and vehicles, the city becomes somewhat of a ghost town after midnight. But no matter what time of day or night, taxis and rickshaw-wallahs have an uncanny way of popping up out of the blue, ready to whisk you off to wherever you wish to go. Hang out at an enchanting hybrid pub-leisure-club where a DJ rocks the bar; try a disco with the most advanced laser technology and hydraulic effects; hobnob with the city's beautiful people at an urbane lounge bar; enjoy happy hour with a long list of speciality cocktails. Sex on the Beach, Screwdrivers and similarly seductive beverages replace milky chai and foamy cappuccinos when Delhi gets dark.

SPENDING A NIGHT on the town is also a sensational way to witness Delhi's wildly varied fashion scene, with the most eyebrow-lifting ensembles usually found in the city's hippest bars and nightclubs. This is the domain of Delhi's glam young things: well-heeled women who spend a frightful amount of money on clothing with the sole goal of standing out from the crowd – possibly even making it to page 3 of tomorrow's newspaper.

MEANWHILE, JUST A block or two away, in total contrast to the nightclub scene, you may pass a congregation of middle-aged women wrapped in elegant silk saris, avidly discussing the dance performance they just saw at one of the city's clutch of performing arts venues. But, in keeping with Delhi's dynamic personality, that performance could be anything from classical Indian dance to classical Indian dance meets hip-hop.

THEY SAY YOU haven't experienced a festival until you've experienced a festival in Delhi. So add traditional ceremonies and festivals to the entertainment options, and Delhi is unquestionably a city of immense variety and jaw-dropping contrasts.

72.

FESTIVE FLOURISHES *

{ * **DIWALI, THE FESTIVAL OF LIGHTS, IS THE EVENT OF THE YEAR.** The city twinkles }
with oil lamps, lit to show Lord Rama the way home from exile, and festive meals and
gifts are produced. Also prominent on the festival calendar is Holi, an adrenaline-
pumping festival known for the mischievous pelting of gulal (coloured powder) and
water. Holi celebrates the arrival of spring and the death of the demoness Holika in late
February or early March. It's a celebration of joy and hope and ritualistic bonfires are
lit on the eve of the first day.

IN A DIFFERENT SPHERE, 26 January 1950 is one of the most important days in
Indian history. The constitution of India came into force on this day and the country
became a republic, realising the dreams of Mahatma Gandhi and the numerous
freedom fighters who tought for independence. Republic Day is celebrated each year
with solemn pomp and pageantry, culminating with a spectacular military procession
known as the Beating of the Retreat and a cultural extravaganza, in which every state
performs its traditional music and dance.

JEWELS TO JOOTIS*

{ * **WHETHER IT'S JOSTLING WITH THE HOI POLLOI THROUGH ONE OF THE OLD CITY'S CRUSTY BAZAARS,** haggling over the price of a pair of jootis (beaded shoes) or taking a languid look at designer salwar kameez boutiques in the stylish Santushti Complex, you'll find the most stunning arrays of things to buy in Delhi. Orissan trinkets, Rajasthani puppets, Hyderabadi pearls and home-grown bellybutton bindis – they're all here. And then there's the eye-popping contrasts: you can browse for the latest Indian ready-to-wear at a snooty shopping enclave in the morning – rubbing shoulders over blueberry pancakes with Delhi's elite – then spend the afternoon sniffing out spices to make the perfect biryani at the Old City's rough-and-tumble spice market. }

IF AT ANY TIME you feel you're about to drop while you shop, simply slip into the closest sari shop, where sari after sari will be enthusiastically flung out as you cool your heels over a garam garam chai.

SARIS & SINGLETS *

{ * **WELCOME TO 21ST-CENTURY DELHI, WHERE WOMEN COCOONED IN CHIFFON SARIS WALK SIDE BY SIDE WITH GIRLS** wearing hipster jeans and belly-flashing singlet tops. Jeans and T-shirts often outnumber saris and salwar kameez in middle-to upper-class suburbs; some political parties have pointed the finger at American soap operas for brainwashing young women into dressing provocatively, with some even lobbying to ban such shows. Their cries seem to have fallen on deaf ears, judging from the boutiques springing up to meet the city's appetite for fresh designs. }

THE SARI AND SALWAR KAMEEZ are making a big comeback with a funky twist. What's life without a twist, after all? The flesh-revealing backless choli (sari blouse) has become the ultimate fashion statement in certain high-society circles, while salwar kameez in crepe or georgette – with fine prints, glorious colours and raised embroidery – offer both evening glamour and the daytime convenience of the trouser suit.

NIGHT MOVES*

{ * **FIVE-STAR HOTELS TRANSFORM FROM BARS TO NIGHTCLUBS AS THE EVENING UNFOLDS, OFTEN WITH LIVE BANDS.** Some have specific themes along with the music, such as Egyptian. There are come-alive mannequins of Marilyn Monroe at one hotel. Bars that have a pool table or a mixture of hi-tech gizmos are always favourites. There are places where you can join the nouveaux riches, take in an afternoon jam session, or soak up the sounds and sights of an Irish pub and sample its grand collection of single malts, Guinness and Kilkenny. }

FOR A CHANGE from the techno-savvy discos, there are old-world watering holes with bric-a-brac and private hideaways. Other joints offer a dash of bhangra (rhythmic Punjabi music) and filmi (Indian movie music) along with golden oldies, or pick up on retro '70s and '80s Bollywood tunes. And for those who prefer the aroma of brewing coffee, paintings on walls, objets d'art on shelves, that's cool too. There's no end to the variety.

THE ART OF RHYTHM*

{ *** BHARATANATYAM MEETS BALLET IN TODAY'S DYNAMIC PERFORMING ARTS SCENE, WITH RENDITIONS OF SWAN LAKE** taking on an entirely different flavour when blended with a dash of traditional Indian dance and a pinch of sitar. Delivering hit-and-miss results, Delhi's innovative fusion (some say con-fusion!) may not rock everyone's world but it certainly fires the imagination and gets a resounding round of applause for originality. }

THOSE MORE INCLINED to classical music and dance will find no dearth of venues, with the capital city attracting artists from around India. There are two main styles of traditional dance: classical and folk. Classical includes bharatanatyam, kathak, kathakali and Odissi, while folk ranges from the high-spirited bhangra of Punjab to the graceful fishers' dance of Orissa. Classical music falls into two major forms: Hindustani (characteristic of North India) and Carnatic (characteristic of South India), with a potpourri of regional variations within these.

87.

90.

GOLD STAR

DELHI GETS A BIG FAT GOLD STAR FOR ITS TANTALISING SHOPPING OPPORTUNITIES. IT HAS EVERYTHING FROM MEDIEVAL-FLAVOURED MARKETS TO CHICHI SHOPPING ENCLAVES. YOU CAN FIND ITEMS FROM ALL OVER INDIA: WHETHER IT'S PAINTED PAPIER-MÂCHÉ EGGS FROM KASHMIR, KARNATAKAN SANDALWOOD CARVINGS, MIRRORED BEDSPREADS FROM GUJARAT, OR CURLY-TOED RAJASTHANI JOOTIS, DELHI DELIVERS.

MY PERFECT DAY

SARINA SINGH

{ * Peruse the gleaming shops of colonnaded Connaught Place, the city's circle-shaped heart, making sure not to miss the excellent handicraft-filled government and state emporiums that fringe the Big Circle's southern outskirts. After fuelling up on mint chutney sandwiches and freshly brewed coffee at one of Connaught Place's perky little cafés, jump into an autorickshaw and plunge into the raw hullabaloo of Shahjahanabad, the erstwhile walled city, situated just a few kilometres away. Kick off your Old City tour at the 17th-century Red Fort, and follow it up with a visit to the subcontinent's largest mosque, the supremely majestic Jama Masjid. From the mosque, wend your way through the people-packed bazaars of the rambunctious Old City, which offer everything from nose-numbing spices and oil-drenched pickles to jingle-jangling bangles and shiny silver toe-rings. Grab a bite to eat at Old Delhi's Karim's restaurant, which has been dishing out sublime Mughlai cuisine since 1913. After adequately filling your belly, bid farewell to the frazzling Old City and ramble around central Delhi's historic Purana Qila before visiting the blissfully serene Crafts Museum, where you can wander through exhibit-filled galleries and watch visiting artisans turn mud into masterpieces.

AFTER FINISHING A BUSINESS DEGREE IN MELBOURNE, SARINA BOUGHT A ONE-WAY TICKET TO DELHI, WHERE SHE COMPLETED A CORPORATE TRAINEESHIP WITH THE SHERATON. She later swapped hotels for newspapers, working as a freelance journalist and foreign correspondent, writing about everything from economics to fashion. After four years in Delhi she returned to Australia and wrote/directed *Beyond The Royal Veil*, a documentary about contemporary Indian 'royalty'. Sarina has worked on almost 20 Lonely Planet books, including five editions of *India*. She has also written for various international publications such as *National Geographic Traveler* and the *Sunday Times* and is the author of *Polo in India*.

PHOTO CREDITS

CITIESCAPE
DELHI

OCTOBER 2006

**PUBLISHED BY LONELY PLANET
PUBLICATIONS PTY LTD**
ABN 36 005 607 983
90 Maribyrnong St, Footscray,
Victoria 3011, Australia
www.lonelyplanet.com

Printed through Colorcraft Ltd, Hong Kong.
Printed in China.

PHOTOGRAPHS
Many of the images in this book are available
for licensing from Lonely Planet Images.
www.lonelyplanetimages.com

ISBN 1 74104 936 9

LONELY PLANET OFFICES
AUSTRALIA Locked Bag 1, Footscray, Victoria 3011
Telephone 03 8379 8000 Fax 03 8379 8111
Email talk2us@lonelyplanet.com.au
USA 150 Linden St, Oakland, CA 94607
Telephone 510 893 8555 TOLL FREE 800 275 8555
Fax 510 893 8572 Email info@lonelyplanet.com
UK 72–82 Rosebery Ave, London EC1R 4RW
Telephone 020 7841 9000 Fax 020 7841 9001
Email go@lonelyplanet.co.uk

Publisher ROZ HOPKINS
Commissioning Editor ELLIE COBB
Editors JOCELYN HAREWOOD, VANESSA BATTERSBY
Design MARK ADAMS
Layout Designer INDRA KILFOYLE
Image Researcher PEPI BLUCK
Pre-press Production GERARD WALKER
Project Managers ANNELIES MERTENS, ADAM MCCROW
Publishing Planning Manager JO VRACA
Print Production Manager GRAHAM IMESON